The story of Kentucky

Rice S. Eubank

Alpha Editions

This edition published in 2024

ISBN : 9789362921963

Design and Setting By
Alpha Editions
www.alphaedis.com
Email - info@alphaedis.com

As per information held with us this book is in Public Domain.
This book is a reproduction of an important historical work. Alpha Editions uses the best technology to reproduce historical work in the same manner it was first published to preserve its original nature. Any marks or number seen are left intentionally to preserve its true form.

Contents

Geography and First White Visitor .... - 1 -

The Virginians and Daniel Boone .... - 2 -

Beginnings of Settlements .... - 5 -

How the Pioneers Lived and Fought .... - 8 -

George Rogers Clark and the Revolution .... - 11 -

Later Days of Famous Pioneers .... - 14 -

After the Revolution .... - 16 -

Progress .... - 18 -

Early Schools and the First Seminary .... - 19 -

State Government and Foreign Intrigue .... - 20 -

Indian Wars and War of 1812 .... - 22 -

Internal Improvements .... - 23 -

Kentucky and Slavery .... - 24 -

The Civil War and Later .... - 27 -

Geography and First White Visitor

Lying west of the Allegheny Mountains and extending westward for some three hundred miles, bounded, for the most part, on the north by the Ohio River and extending to the Mississippi, lies the State of Kentucky. In its eastern portion, constituting nearly one-third of its area, the surface is broken, and so high as to be termed mountainous. A large area occupying the central third, and in the early day mostly a prairie land, is now known as the famous Blue Grass section. The western third of the State is practically level, being but a few feet above the sea, and cypress swamps are not infrequent. This section is commonly termed "The Pennyrile."

In the middle of the eighteenth century, Kentucky was a portion of that unexplored western realm belonging by grant to the State of Virginia, and designated as a part of Fincastle County. The eastern portion in the early day abounded in wild game common to the Appalachian forests. The undulating grass lands in the central part of the State provided ample grazing for the herds of buffalo and deer that were found there at the time of the coming of man. The skeletons that have been exhumed indicate that it was the feeding ground of the giant mastodon before the discovery of America.

About two hundred years after Columbus discovered America, a young man twenty-two years of age came to Canada from the Old World. On his arrival he learned from the settlers and Indians the possibility of a passage to the South Sea, which they then thought the Gulf of Mexico to be. Desirous of making this journey, and lured by the possibility of reaching the Pacific by water, he secured the assistance of Indians and some white hunters as guides and set out upon an expedition of exploration into the country concerning which he had heard such fascinating stories.

Crossing the St. Lawrence and traveling southward, he came to what is now called Allegheny River. Securing birchbark canoes, he and his party descended the Allegheny to its junction with the Monongahela, then turning southwestward on the beautiful stream formed by these two small rivers and now known as the Ohio, he explored the country along the banks of the river to what was called by him the Rapids of the Ohio. Thus, LaSalle was the first to gaze upon the country from the mouth of the Big Sandy to the present site of Louisville, and to make a record of such discoveries.

The Virginians and Daniel Boone

Near the middle of the eighteenth century, or about 1750, a party of Virginia hunters, growing weary of the monotony of home life and desiring to find better hunting grounds, penetrated the Appalachian Mountains by way of Powell's Valley and through Cumberland Gap, into the eastern portion of what is now Kentucky, and hence were the first white men to approach the land from the eastern side. In 1767, John Finley and Daniel Boone, hearing of the fine hunting in this section, came to Kentucky from North Carolina and built a cabin on Red River, near where Estill, Powell, and Clark counties are now joined. Two years later, about forty hunters and adventurers came to the territory and made their camp at what they then called Price's Meadows, about six miles from the present site of Monticello in Wayne County. This camp, by virtue of its location near the Cumberland River, developed into a distributing point for the country lying along the Cumberland, now included in Wayne, Green, Barren and Warren counties. Another station was built near Greensburg. These stations or camps seem to have served only the immediate needs of the hunters while they were in the territory.

Daniel Boone

Daniel Boone seems to have been the only one of these hunters to whom the wilderness especially appealed. Consequently, for many years he made frequent trips into the territory, staying as long as two years on one occasion, and winning the title of The Long Hunter. Boone was alone on many of these trips, never seeing the face of a white man, but frequently meeting roving bands of Indians. From a cave in the side of Pilot Knob in Powell County, he could catch glimpses of the joyous sports of the

Shawnee boys at Indian Fields; and from the projecting rocks he feasted his eyes on the herds of buffalo winding across the prairie.

No permanent Indian villages were found in Kentucky. It seems to have been a choice bit of hunting ground strongly contested by the tribes of the North and the tribes of the South. The Shawnees had a village at Indian Fields, in the eastern portion of Clark County, near the beautiful stream called Lulbegrud Creek.

Boone seems to have been endowed with the faculty that enabled him to pass, in his first years of wandering, from tribe to tribe; and from these Indians he learned that the common name of the country, known to all, was Kan-tuckee (kane-tooch-ee), so called by the Indians because of the abundance of a peculiar reed growing along the river, now known as pipe-stem cane.

Boone remained in the wilderness so long that his brother and a searching party came to find him. They found him in good health and spirits, enjoying life, and living in peace with the Indian tribes. The party, with Boone, returned to the valley of the Yadkin, and told such stories of the enchanted land as caused the settlers of the region to listen eagerly, and to feel the stirring of the pioneer spirit. Not caring for the growing crops and with no relish for the monotonous labor, Boone easily persuaded a company of men to come with him to the wilderness and to bring their families.

Boone's Trail

The journey was tedious. Those on foot went ahead and blazed a trail for the few wagons, pack horses and domestic animals, and killed game to furnish meat when the next camp should be struck at nightfall. It was a courageous, jolly party that thus marched through Cumberland Gap, and blazed a way which has since been known as Boone's Trail. Hostile Indians had to be fought along the way, and several of the party were slain, among them being Boone's son. An Englishman, also, was killed, and his young son was adopted by Boone and thereafter known as his own son.

Beginnings of Settlements

The party passed the present site of Richmond in Madison County, and reached a point on the Kentucky River, in 1775, where Boonesborough was built. The site selected was a broad, level stretch of land, with the river to the north, and high hills to the south. This particular spot was selected because of a fine spring of water, and high hills that could be used for sentinel towers, inclosing fine level ground for cultivation. The settlers cut trees and constructed a stockade in the form of a hollow square. It was from this fort that Rebecca Boone and the Calloway girls were stolen by Indians while boating on the Kentucky River.

Boone's Fort

About the same time that Boonesborough was being established, Captain James Harrod with a party of forty men descended the Ohio River, stopped for a time at the mouth of Licking River, and felled some trees on the present site of Cincinnati. Not being satisfied with the location of the settlement, they followed the Ohio to the mouth of the Kentucky River and ascended the Kentucky to a spot now known as Oregon Landing.

Being fatigued from their long and difficult voyage, they left their boats and took a course from the river and found a big spring at which they built a stockade on the present site of Harrodsburg.

The large flowing spring one mile west of the present town of Stanford, Lincoln County, was made the site of a third settlement. Capt. Benjamin Logan headed this party of pioneers, and the station was, for a time, known as Logan's Fort. Afterward, because of the fact that the fort was made by planting logs on end, it was called Standing Fort, and in later years the town was called Stanford. In the Logan party was a priest who was a musician of rare ability. In his daily walks, he was accustomed to sit, meditating, at the mouth of the cave from which ran the water of this great spring. The ripple of the stream flowing from the cavern, over the rocks and through the spearmint, was music to the Father's ear, and to him it seemed the spirit of St. Asaph, the director of King David's choir. He it was who named the spring and the creek which flows from it, St. Asaph's.

While the people busied themselves at Harrodsburg, Boonesborough and Logan's Fort, Simon Kenton, disappointed in a love affair in Virginia, seeking relief from sorrow by satisfying his hunger for hunting and at the same time acting in the interest of Lord Dunmore, came to Kentucky. He reached a point near Old Washington in Mason County, where he and his party cleared an acre of land, planted corn and ate the roasting ears the same summer. So far as we know, this was the first agricultural activity in the Commonwealth.

In April, 1775, the first battle of the Revolutionary War was fought at Lexington, Mass. At that time a party of hunters was camped at the big spring near the present site of the Fayette County courthouse, in Lexington, Ky. Months later, the news of the American victory reached the settlers, and because of their great joy over the victory gained, they named the camp site Lexington.

Limestone (now Maysville), Royal Springs (now Georgetown) and Martin's Station were also built this year.

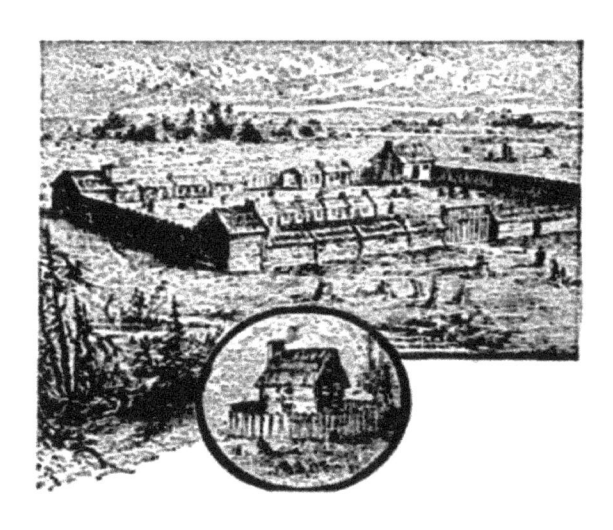

Stockade and Cabins at Lexington

In 1779, Lexington was first permanently improved and cabins built. From these rude stockade cabins grew the beautiful city of the Blue Grass, in which town for many years were manufactured practically all the fur hats worn in the Ohio and Mississippi valleys. Being in the center of the hemp-growing section, practically all the ropes and cables used in boating on the Ohio, Mississippi and Kentucky rivers were made in Lexington. These commercial enterprises, together with the exceptional fertility of the soil, account for the development of the city of Lexington more rapidly than the surrounding forts and stations.

Daniel Boone was consulted regarding the advisability of the location of all settlements made during the early days, because he knew the country better than any other one person, and knew the wilderness as few have known it.

Hunters and trappers began to traffic along the Ohio River, and supplies for the more northern settlements were shipped on the Ohio and unloaded at Limestone or at The Rapids. At this latter point it was necessary, if supplies were sent farther down the stream, to unload and carry them to a point below the rapids, when the boats would have to be launched again and reloaded. This necessitated a delay, especially as the traders soon fell upon the plan of having one line of boats plying above the rapids and another plying between points below the rapids. Men for unloading and loading were kept always on the ground. This little settlement became permanent, and is now the largest town in the State—Louisville.

How the Pioneers Lived and Fought

First Stockade and Cabins at the Falls of Ohio, now Louisville. Built by George Rogers Clark in 1776.

After the wives of the settlers in the various forts came to Kentucky, home life took on the appearance of a settled community. Homes were built outside the stockades, nearly every man of family had a farm of his own, land was cleared, fruit trees were set out, attention was given to the raising of hogs, sheep, cattle and horses, and a little Empire of the West began to appear. The women were busy with spinning, weaving and general housework. The men cleared and fenced their land. The fortifications were kept only as a refuge in time of an attack by the Indians—which, however, was not infrequent, because the French in the North coveted the rich lands beyond the Alleghenies, and incited the Indians to warfare against the white people who were settling there. It was the sturdy pioneers of Kentucky, acting in the name of Virginia, who held the frontier against the encroachments of the French, as the property of the English crown.

The notorious renegade, Simon Girty, a white man who for certain reasons forsook civilized society and associated himself with the Indians of Northern Ohio, was willing at all times to harass the settlers on the frontier at the suggestion of the French military commanders. This man cared not for spilling the blood of his own race, and frequently would lead his hostile bands in attacks against the unprotected settlements. His favorite time for attack seemed to be in the spring of the year, when the men were at work in the fields and offered the least resistance by a speedy rally of forces.

We have noticed that all these forts were built near a spring of unfailing water. The pioneers seem always to have left the spring outside the inclosure, however, and since this worked a great hardship in time of siege, it seems to have been bad judgment. Girty's Indians attacked Logan's Fort. The supply of water inside the fort was exhausted, and the suffering was intense. After this siege, General Logan decided never again to be subjected to such an extremity. He could not bring the spring to the fort, and it was also difficult to transplant the fort. So he summoned the settlers and proposed a plan to which they agreed. The hours when they were not working in the fields or building new cabins they spent in digging, until a tunnel was made from the stockade to the spring. In succeeding attacks, the General had his granaries and storehouses well supplied with food and ammunition, and it was an easy matter to send a boy with a bucket through the tunnel to the spring for water. This precaution on the part of the General prevented exhaustion during the next attack on Logan's Fort. The Indians, unable to understand how the settlers in the fort could do so long without water, supposed them to be miraculously defended by the Great Spirit, and never afterward could Girty lead his band to attack Logan's Fort.

The settlers at Bryan's Station, a few miles from Lexington, did not take a similar precaution. During one of the Indian attacks on them the supply of water in the fort became exhausted, and surrender seemed unavoidable. The women of the fort volunteered to go for water, and taking buckets marched down to the spring. The Indians were surprised, superstitious, and panic-stricken, and refused to fire on them. The women filled their buckets and returned in safety to the stockade.

Notwithstanding the bounteous provision made by Nature to supply the needs of the settler in the way of fruits, wild meats, and skins for clothing, life in the settlements was plain in the extreme. Furniture and household utensils were scant and crude, for the most part being of home construction. Salt was one of the greatest needs of the settlers. At first, they made it from the water of the numerous salt licks, each family making its supply by boiling the water in a kettle until the moisture had evaporated, leaving the salt encrusted in the kettle. These kettles were crude, and invariably small. Hence it was more difficult to supply a family with salt than with sugar, which was easily made by boiling down the sap from the maple trees. After awhile, the Virginia authorities sent out a number of large kettles and two expert salt makers, who reported to Captain Boone for service. Boone, with his two experts and thirty other men, left Boonesborough for the Lower Blue Lick Spring, fifty or more miles toward the north. Here they made a camp and set to work to manufacture a stock of salt sufficient to supply the needs of all the settlements for a period of twelve months. From time to time a small party was sent back to the different forts with packhorses laden with salt. On their return, they would bring supplies, parched corn, and perhaps a few of the simple comforts that seemed almost luxuries to the hardy backwoodsmen. Meat constituted the chief article of diet for the workers of the salt factory. It required no small amount to satisfy the appetites of thirty vigorous men. Boone, as the most expert hunter among them, undertook to supply the camp with meat. The task was, to him, a thoroughly congenial one, which we cannot imagine the more civilized task of manufacturing salt to have been.

It was Boone's custom to go out some miles from camp every morning, returning at the close of the day with as much game as he could carry, and often leaving a quantity at a particular spot to be sent for with a packhorse. One afternoon Boone was making his way toward the salt works after a day of successful hunting, when he suddenly found himself surrounded by a company of Indians. Not having seen a redskin for months, and believing it unlikely that they could be present in large numbers at that time of the year, Boone was not as keenly on the alert as usual. The savages had found Boone's trail while wandering through the woods. He was taken captive, adopted into the tribe, his hair picked out in Indian fashion, and the war paint added. Boone's failure to return led the men in the camp to suspect the presence of Indians, and to guess that Boone had fallen captive. The alarm was quickly sent to the surrounding forts. Maj. Harlan, Col. Trigg, Col. Todd, and Boone's brother led a body of men against the Indians in what proved to be the bloodiest battle recorded in the annals of the territory, and known as the Battle of Blue Licks. In this battle, Boone's eldest son was slain, and it is said the old man never could refer to the battle without shedding tears. In the midst of the battle, Boone escaped from his captors and rejoined the settlers.

George Rogers Clark and the Revolution

Among the many men of sterling quality who for various reasons came out to Kentucky, was one stalwart, well-trained, military genius known in history as General George Rogers Clark. His first trip to Kentucky was semi-official, as a representative of the Virginia Legislature, to visit the various forts and settlements and to report progress to the state government. He found the settlers in dire need of powder. Reporting this to the Virginia authorities, he succeeded in securing for the settlers a quantity, which was yet insufficient to defend them against the Indians.

George Rogers Clark

Of Clark's second appearance in Kentucky, General Ray, who was at that time a boy of sixteen, living at Harrodsburg (or Harrod's Station as it was then called), gives the following account: "I had come down to where I now live, about four miles from Harrodsburg, to turn some horses on the range. I had killed a small blue-winged duck that was feeding in my spring, and had roasted it nicely by a fire on the brow of the hill. While waiting for the duck to cool, I was startled by the sudden appearance of a fine, soldierly-looking man. 'How do you do, my little fellow? What is your name? Aren't you afraid of being in the woods by yourself?' Answering his inquiries, I invited him to partake of my duck, which he did, without leaving me a bone to pick, his appetite was so keen. Had I known him then as I did afterwards, he would have been welcome to all the game I could have killed. Having devoured my duck, he asked me questions about the settlers, the Indians and the condition of affairs in the locality." These the boy answered as well as he could, and then ventured to ask the name of his guest. "My name is Clark," was the response, "and I have come out here to see how you brave fellows are doing in Kentucky, and to lend you a helping hand, if necessary."

With the universal consent of the settlers, Clark naturally assumed the military leadership of the territory, visiting all the fortifications, looking after their military stores, drilling the men, and otherwise strengthening the defenses of the pioneers. Clark made other trips to Virginia in behalf of the frontiersmen, but since the resources of Virginia were severely taxed by the necessary support given to the other colonies during the Revolutionary War, he received little or no encouragement, and practically nothing in the way of military supplies. It is stated that he provided the necessities at his own expense, defraying the cost of transportation and distribution. Later, powder was made by the settlers of Kentucky by leaching saltpetre from the soil in various sections and combining it with charcoal and other ingredients.

The English army officers formed alliances with the Indian tribes living north of the Ohio River in the territory now composing Ohio, Indiana and Illinois and incited them to frequent attacks on the Kentucky settlements, with the hope that they would the sooner capture the State of Virginia by an approach from the west. Clark, as military commander of Kentucky, sent spies into this northern country to determine the location of the fortresses and the number of English and Indians in each. One of these spies was the celebrated Simon Kenton, who was not content with locating the enemy but attempted to recapture a lot of horses stolen from Kentucky by the Indians on a former raid. Kenton and his companions were not able to travel fast with the number of horses they had secured, and when they were attacked by a band of Indians, Kenton's companions were slain and he was captured. The Indians hated him cordially and began to beat him unmercifully, calling him the "hoss-steal." They easily could have murdered Kenton on the spot, but since he had proved such a terrible foe to them in the past, they preferred to enjoy their capture all the more by torturing him for awhile. He was carried by the Indians to Chillicothe, where he was several times forced to run the gauntlet. Finally, when tied to the stake to be burned, he was recognized by his boyhood friend, Simon Girty, who sent him to Detroit, from which place he made his escape and returned to Kentucky, reporting to General Clark the conditions as he had found them.

Other spies returned, and from the general reports General Clark thought it necessary to make another appeal to Virginia for aid. In 1778, Governor Patrick Henry of Virginia gave to Clark a commission as commanding officer to take such soldiers as he could secure in Virginia, together with his Kentuckians, and go against the British and Indians north of the Ohio River. Leaving Corn Island, now Louisville, he and his brave followers marched northward through swamps and swam streams, capturing every fortification to which they came. Among these were Kaskaskia and Vincennes. By this heroic deed of Clark's the great territory north of the Ohio River was secured from the British, and became a part of Virginia's territory. Clark continued at the head of military affairs in Kentucky, but his greatest work was done before he was thirty years of age.

Later Days of Famous Pioneers

When peace came, Clark settled about eight miles from Louisville and fell into habits of intemperance which unfitted him for public service. He was given large land bounties by Virginia, in recognition of services rendered, but conflicting claims prevented him coming into possession of the land for years, thus leaving him helpless and poor in his old age. The Virginia legislature voted him a jeweled sword, which was sent to the old man by a special messenger. When the young man made his speech presenting the sword, Clark replied, "Young man, go tell Virginia, when she needed a sword I found one. Now, I need bread." The worn-out old soldier lived only a little while longer, and in 1818 died and was buried at Locust Grove, Ky. It has been said that a French officer who met Clark at Yorktown, on his return to France, said to the king: "Sire, there are two Washingtons in America." "What do you mean?" said the king. "I mean," said the officer, "that there is Washington whom the world knows; and there is George Rogers Clark, the conqueror of the Northwest, as great a man as Washington in his field of action and for his opportunity."

Simon Kenton shared a like fate. Losing his land, acre by acre, this simple-hearted old pioneer found himself penniless in his old age. He was then allowed by law, to the shame of all civilization, to be cast into prison for debt upon the same spot upon which he had built his first cabin in 1775. In 1799, as a beggar, he moved into Ohio. In 1813, he joined Governor Shelby's troops and was with them in the Battle of the Thames. In 1820, this poor old man moved to a site on Scioto river, where the Indians forty years before had tied him to a stake to be burned. Near the close of his life he was given some mountain lands and a small pension.

Daniel Boone lost all his fine lands in Kentucky, also, and came to such poverty as to lead him in one of his petitions to say, "I have not a spot of ground whereon to lay my bones." He left Kentucky, saying he would never return to live in a country so ungrateful. About 1796 he moved to Missouri and settled fifty miles from St. Louis. Spain owned that territory then, and the Spanish government gave him a liberal grant of land. Around him his sons and daughters and their families settled. The broad forests were full of game, and here Boone again indulged his passion for a hunter's life. The old hunter neglected to complete his titles to his new lands, and these he also lost. Congress afterward made him a smaller grant. He died in Missouri in 1820, at the age of eighty-six, and was buried in a coffin which he had made for himself some years before. In 1845, the Legislature of Kentucky had the remains of the pioneer and his wife removed and buried with honor in the cemetery at Frankfort. A suitable monument was erected to mark their resting place.

In the early days of the settlement of Kentucky, all men were not engaged in fighting Indians, building forts and clearing ground. On the contrary, the fertility of the soil and the wealth of timber and mineral led men to look to the commercial value of real estate, and consequently there was formed a powerful company known as The Transylvania Land Company, which had for its purpose the ownership and control of the valuable lands. Judge Richard Henderson, a native of Virginia, was the leader in the formation of this Company.

Taking advantage of the unsettled boundaries west of the mountains and knowing that the several states claimed the country by right of grants from the kings of the countries of Europe, the Transylvania Company attempted to organize the territory into a separate government. These men gave the settlers no little worry over the ownership of their lands, and because Virginia was engaged in the War of the Revolution little attention was paid to affairs in Kentucky. Finally, in 1776, the settlers in Kentucky called a meeting at Harrodsburg and sent Gabriel Jones and George Rogers Clark to the Legislature of Virginia with a statement that unless Virginia should protect the settlers against the Transylvania Company and others, the people would organize the territory into a separate government, and take their place among the States. To this statement the Virginia Legislature gave heed, and cut off from Fincastle County, Virginia, all that unsurveyed territory west of the Allegheny Mountains, and organized it into the County of Kentucky, as a part of Virginia. This act enabled the settlers to have a regular form of county government with a sheriff and other county officials, as well as two representatives in the Virginia Assembly.

Things went well in the new county for awhile. Agriculture was engaged in more extensively and the good work of developing the country went steadily on, interrupted all too frequently by the attacks of the Indians from the north, in very much the same manner as before, though less frequently.

People in the eastern colonies heard of the fertility of the soil and of the many attractive features of the country, and as a result large numbers from all the older settlements determined to try their fortunes in the favored land. Population increased to such an extent that it was thought advisable to divide the territory into three counties (Jefferson, Lincoln and Fayette), and courts were established.

After the Revolution

The treaty of peace which ended the War of the Revolution was concluded in November, 1782, but the people of Kentucky did not get the news for nearly four months later. All were rejoiced that the struggle was ended and confidently expected that trouble with the Indians would cease, since there seemed no further reason for inciting them to make war on the Kentuckians. The people were doomed to disappointment. The treaty left possessions so poorly defined that not only did the Indians make occasional invasions into the territory to plunder, under the direction of the military commanders of the north, but the people were threatened by a still graver danger. The unsettled boundaries and titles of lands along the Mississippi River caused a question of ownership to arise between France, England and Spain. Spain at that time controlled the lower Mississippi River, and men from that country secretly came to Kentucky attempting to arouse the people to the act of establishing a separate nation under the protection of Spain. The loyalty of the good men of Kentucky to the rights of Virginia cannot be too highly praised. There were some persons, though, who for glory and private gain did all in their power to stir up the rebellion and to establish a separate government. Kentucky was virtually left to her fate beyond the mountains during the trying times following the close of the Revolution.

The needs of the territory and the constant menace from these Spanish agents led the better class of men in Kentucky to consider the question of asking Virginia to be allowed the privilege of separation, with the expectation of the territory's being formed into a State, equal with others of the Union. This would give a better administration of affairs and would put an end to the efforts of agents from other countries desiring to establish a separate nation.

On May 23, 1785, a convention of delegates met at Danville and sent the following resolution to the Virginia Assembly: "Resolved: That it is the duty of the convention, as they regard the prosperity and happiness of their constituents, to pray the General Assembly at the ensuing session for an act to separate this district from the present government, on terms honorable to both and injurious to neither, in order that it may enjoy all the advantages and rights of a free, sovereign and independent republic."

In 1786, Virginia passed the act providing for the separation of Kentucky, but she made it conditional on the willingness of the Congress of the United States to admit Kentucky as one of the States of the Union, and upon the willingness of Kentucky to become a member of the Union as soon as separated from Virginia, thus preventing Kentucky from becoming an independent republic, or a part of any foreign nation. It was during these days that enemies to both Kentucky and the nation were busiest in their efforts secretly to plan for either an independent government or an alliance with Spain. Kentucky became a State in 1792, being the fifteenth in the Union.

Progress

While the preceding pages have dealt largely with the struggle for existence in the frontier country, it must not be understood that during these years the entire attention of the settlers was given to waging war against the Indians. The Indian invasions were altogether too frequent, and their savage cruelty entirely too terrible to be mentioned here, and this continued for many years after the country was supposed to be entirely free from terrors of the sort. Yet the people had all the while been doing remarkably well, not only in their efforts to conquer the wilderness, but to establish a civilization which compared favorably with the progress made in the more settled sections of our country at that time.

The question of land titles offered a fine field for litigation, and among the brilliant lawyers attracted to the country was Henry Clay of Virginia, who in his twenty-fifth year was elected to the State Legislature of Kentucky, and at thirty was a United States Senator. From this period, with but few brief intervals, his long life was spent in the public service, and in the highest positions within the gift of the people. It was he who said, "I would rather be right than be President."

In 1787, there was established at Lexington The Kentucky Gazette, by John Bradford. This was the first newspaper to be published west of the Allegheny Mountains. Since they had no rural delivery in those days the paper was sometimes weeks old before the people received it. It was practically the only medium for the general dissemination of knowledge throughout the settlements. With great eagerness would the people of any particular section assemble at their fort, store or tavern, on "paper day," and the brightest youngster or the most accomplished reader in the community would delight his auditors by reading aloud the things that had happened in the world at large, the colonies in general, and in Kentucky in particular.

Early Schools and the First Seminary

At this early date, schools were established in Kentucky and taught in the stockade forts. A Mrs. Coons "kept" school at Harrod's Station; John May at McAfee, and a Mr. Doniphan at Boonesborough. Later, log cabin school houses were built farther out into the settlements. The school boys were required to carry guns with them to school, that they might be ready to meet any danger. School books were rare and very expensive. The diligent teacher would copy from his rare and expensive texts lessons to be learned in the subject of arithmetic and other branches, often one copy serving a whole family. In 1798, local school books appeared. The Kentucky Primer and The Kentucky Speller were printed at Washington, the old county seat of Mason county, and Harrison's Grammar was printed at Frankfort in the same year.

Twenty thousand acres of land were given by Virginia for the establishment of Transylvania Seminary in 1783. Its first principal was the Rev. David Rice, a pioneer Presbyterian preacher and a graduate of Princeton University. In 1787 the institution was moved from near Danville to Lexington. George Washington contributed liberally to the maintenance of this school, and Lafayette, on his return to America, visited the school and made a donation to its support. From this seminary grew the now famous Transylvania University, Lexington, Ky.

In 1798 the Legislature of Kentucky donated six thousand acres of land to each county then in existence, for the purpose of establishing county seminaries. In many sections of the state these old pioneer buildings of brick and stone may be seen today. These institutions did much for education in their time.

Our Commonwealth had, even at this early period, produced an unusual number of inventors of note. John Fitch, in 1786, first successfully applied steam as a motor power to passenger boats. James Rumsey, the same year, propelled a boat with steam. Edward West, in 1794, constructed a model boat and propelled it by steam, on Elkhorn Creek, near Lexington. He later invented the nail-cutting machine which made it possible to cut nails rapidly from wrought iron, whereas they had formerly been hammered out by hand. Thomas H. Barlow invented the Planetarium, an instrument by which the movements of the earth and moon around the sun were shown.

State Government and Foreign Intrigue

Isaac Shelby, a native of Maryland, but who had spent his early life in North Carolina with the frontiersmen, fighting the Indians and rendering valiant service in the War of the Revolution, after the conclusion of peace with England had come to Kentucky in 1783. He, like Clark, was a great leader of men. He took an active interest in political, civil, military and social affairs in Kentucky, and was elected the first Governor of the State. On the fourth of June, 1792, the Legislature assembled at Lexington. The chief business of the first Legislature seems to have been the selection of a site for a permanent seat of government, or capital. Frankfort was finally decided upon, and a State House of stone was erected.

Gov. Isaac Shelby

Intrigue on the part of foreign governments, however, did not cease with the organization of State government. The Spanish governor at New Orleans continued to send emissaries into the State, seeking to arouse a spirit of discontent, and if possible bring about a separation of the State from the Union. So successful were these agents that they were able to secure the good will of some men in high places, by paying as high as two thousand dollars a year salary. One Thomas Power seems to have been the most active agent of the Spanish government, and he held out as an inducement the great commercial privileges that would come to Kentucky through the free navigation of the Mississippi River, and he further offered to place two hundred thousand dollars at the disposal of his friends if they would bring about a separation from the nation. These treasonable offers, however, were spurned, with one or two exceptions, by the sturdy and loyal manhood of Kentucky.

After the overtures of the Spanish agents, came the royal offers of an English protectorate, and later the offensive scheme of Genet and his French agents to arm and equip a flotilla of two thousand Kentuckians for the purpose of capturing New Orleans, and thus reopen the Mississippi River for navigation, which had been so profitable to Kentuckians prior to the withdrawal of that privilege by the Spanish government.

In 1805, Aaron Burr, whose term as Vice-President of the United States had expired, became unpopular because of his criticisms of the administration of President Jefferson, and because of his having killed Alexander Hamilton in a duel. Being ambitious, Burr was morbidly restless because of the turn his fortunes had taken. He visited Kentucky and different points between New Orleans and St. Louis. He succeeded in drawing into his plans one Blennerhassett, a wealthy man who lived on a beautiful island in the Ohio River. It is supposed that his plan was to found an empire in the West, and to make himself the ruler of the same. During Burr's visits to Kentucky, it is said that he frequently made his headquarters at an old brick residence in Eddyville, overlooking the Cumberland River. In November, 1806, Burr was brought into court at Frankfort, charged with organizing a military expedition against Mexico. He was defended by Henry Clay and the grand jury failed to indict him. This acquittal was celebrated by a ball at Frankfort. A few months later he was arrested in Alabama, taken to Richmond, Va., and acquitted of treason after a trial lasting six months.

Indian Wars and War of 1812

The great Shawnee chief, Tecumseh, formed a federation of all the northern tribes of Indians for a general massacre of all settlers west of the Alleghenies. Kentucky contributed a great number of soldiers to the army under General William Henry Harrison. This army, with Governor Shelby at the head of the Kentucky brigade, marched against the northern tribes and defeated them at the Battle of Tippecanoe. The fleeing Indians were overtaken at the River Thames, and the cry of the Kentuckians was, "Remember the Raisin and revenge." In this battle, Col. Richard F. Johnson of Kentucky slew the noted chief, Tecumseh.

In the second war between the United States and England, in 1812, Kentuckians took a prominent part in nearly all battles against the British. Especially did they distinguish themselves as expert riflemen at the Battle of New Orleans. Most of the cannon ball used in this battle had been made at the old iron furnace in Bath County, near where Owingsville now stands, and a great portion of the powder had been manufactured from the saltpeter leached from the soil in Mammoth Cave, Edmonson County, Kentucky.

While Kentuckians were winning laurels on the battlefields of the Indian wars and the War of 1812, literary pursuits were not neglected. In 1785, John Filson wrote the first history of the State, and drew maps of the region. In 1812, Humphrey Marshall, Sr., also wrote a history of Kentucky. Colleges were being established, and young men were being trained in classical lore and oratory. Among the prominent orators of the early day were Thomas F. Marshall and Richard M. Menefee. The genius, ready wit, satire, and forensic power of Marshall made him a favorite with all audiences at all times; but unfortunately his habit of intemperance lessened his powers and closed his career. The oratory of Menefee was so pleasing and convincing as to cause him to be called the Patrick Henry of the West.

Internal Improvements

The wealth of timber, mineral, and farm products of the State was so great as to cause early improvements in the building of macadamized roads or pikes, and as early as 1830 the turnpike from Maysville to Lexington was built to facilitate the movement of freight and farm products from the bluegrass region to the towns along the Ohio River on the northern boundary. A similar road was built from Louisville through Glasgow and Bowling Green to Nashville, Tenn., and this road not only served as a commercial outlet to the South, but has played an important part in the history and subsequent development of the State.

Early in the past century, interest was shown in the making of the water courses of Kentucky navigable throughout the year by the building of locks and dams. These were built on Kentucky, Barren and Green Rivers. Kentucky is said to have a greater number of miles of navigable streams than is owned by any other State. Its territory was supposed, in the early days, to extend to low water mark on the eastern side of the Big Sandy River, to the northern bank of the Ohio River, and to the western bank of the Mississippi on the western border, while the Kentucky, Barren and Green rivers lie wholly within its borders, and the Cumberland and Tennessee rivers cross the State in the western section. Green River is said to be one of the deepest river waterways in the world, and the scenery along its banks is indeed picturesque. The towering walls on either side of the Kentucky River between Frankfort and Beattyville rival in grandeur and majestic beauty the famous palisades of the Hudson or the castellated southern shore of the beautiful Columbia River.

Railroad construction was early commenced in Kentucky. While traveling from Lexington to Frankfort today over the L. & N. railroad, one can see from the car windows the old grade and the cuts indicating the line along which ran the early cars on stones in which grooves were cut for the guidance of the wheels instead of the steel rail and the flange wheel of the present day. These early cars were drawn by mules, after they had been pulled by a windlass up the cliff from the boat landing at Frankfort. The mules and the rock rails were soon replaced by two locomotives and iron rails. One engine brought the train from Frankfort to a point half way, by noon, and after the passengers had eaten dinner at Midway, the other engine took the train on to Lexington.

Kentucky and Slavery

The early settlers from Virginia brought their slaves with them, and when the State was established, no one thought of abolishing the institution of slavery. The melodious voices of the blacks could be heard in the clearing grounds and the "black mammies" and the little pickaninnies were familiar objects about every well-to-do home. For the most part, the Kentuckian was considerate of the welfare of his slaves, and both master and slave were happy in the olden day. Those who are old enough to remember, can tell some stories of the loyalty of the slave to his master, and of the kindly relationship that existed between the two races. About 1829 there began to develop in the minds of many Kentuckians a sentiment which afterward grew into strong opposition to the state of affairs which made it possible for one man to own the body and control the actions of another. In 1831, Cassius M. Clay, while attending Yale College, became thoroughly aroused to the evils of slavery, and when he returned to Kentucky he began to speak and to write in opposition to the institution. He established a paper in Lexington by means of which he was able to arouse sentiment in support of his contention against slavery. He was probably the first pronounced and powerful abolitionist in the State, and became almost as famous in the South as was William Lloyd Garrison in the North.

The question continued to be one of absorbing interest, and the anti-slavery party gained in strength steadily. When Texas declared her independence from Mexico, and sought admission into the Union of States, the slavery question was discussed in that connection in Kentucky as heatedly as in any other section. General Zachary Taylor, a native Kentuckian, born and reared near Louisville, was placed in command of the American forces when war was about to be declared against Mexico. This and the fact that William O. Butler and Thomas Marshall were commissioned officers under Taylor, and also from Kentucky, served to increase the interest in the approaching struggle with Mexico, and intensified the zeal of both the slavery and the anti-slavery parties. Everywhere the question was, "Shall Texas come to us as a slave or a free state?"

On the third of June, 1808, just about four years before our Kentucky soldiers were called upon to enlist to do battle against the British in the War of 1812, there was born in an old-fashioned log house in that part of Kentucky where the town of Fairview now stands, a boy named Jefferson Davis, who was destined to become one of the conspicuous characters in the nation. As a child, he was mild of manner and rather timid, but possessed a strong and resolute will. He willingly and easily learned the contents of such books as the schools of the time afforded, and at an early age he matriculated as a student at Transylvania Seminary, where he distinguished himself as a gentleman and a scholar. A point of interest in Lexington is the quaint little house where he roomed while he was a student at the Seminary.

The spirit of the times led young Davis to choose a military career, and he entered West Point from which he graduated in 1828. We find him soon as a captain in the regiment commanded by General Zachary Taylor. While stationed at Louisville, he met, wooed, and wed the beautiful daughter of General Taylor—not, however, with the consent and blessing of the General. A pretty story is told of Davis and Taylor concerning their reconciliation. During the Mexican War, Davis commanded a company of artillery. On one occasion, General Taylor ordered Captain Bragg to unlimber and fire at the enemy, and Bragg was disposed to urge the futility of the effort, since it would result in presenting the battery to the Mexicans and he thought there was no hope of holding the position. With the coolness for which he was noted, Captain Davis was seen to wheel his battery into line, and he directed the maneuvres in such manner as soon to be in complete control, and the battle was won. The next morning, says the story, General Taylor sent an orderly to the tent of Captain Davis, commanding him to report at headquarters. The order was obeyed; and when Davis had saluted his superior officer and stood at attention, the crusty old general stepped forward and, with a moistened eye, extended his hand and said, "Captain Davis, my daughter was a better judge of a man than I." They were the warmest friends ever afterward.

Jefferson Davis

While Davis was Secretary of War of the United States, he practically reorganized the army and revised the tactics. After the close of the Mexican War, he became a Congressman from Mississippi, and afterward was sent to the United States Senate from that State. When he resigned his seat in the United States Senate, he delivered a farewell speech setting forth his reasons for so doing. This is said to be one of the greatest addresses ever delivered before the Senate. He was chosen President of the Southern Confederacy at a time when another great Kentuckian, who had been born in the same section of the state, was President of the United States.

In a rude log hut, not many miles from the place where Jefferson Davis first saw the light, was born a boy whom the world has placed on the highest pedestal of fame. Abraham Lincoln was born in Larue County on February 12, 1809; his life is so well known that there is little of it not familiar to the average school boy.

The Civil War and Later

When the Civil War between the States of the Union was about to begin, Kentucky refused to take sides in the controversy, and in the strict sense of the term was never out of the Union. When the President of the United States called on Kentucky to furnish men and equipment for the Union army, the Governor replied that the State was neutral and would take no steps toward secession, nor would it espouse coercion by force of arms. The people, however, chose for themselves, and enlisted in the Union or in the Confederate army, as they believed to be in the right of the controversy. The result was that about an equal number enlisted with both armies. Hence the State became a common battleground during the struggle, very much as it was in the days when the Indian tribes from the North and from the South met on our soil as a common battleground. Families were divided as to their espousal of the respective sides of the contest, father and son frequently taking up arms on opposite sides. When the war closed, the people went to work with a will to repair the damages incident to the struggle, and no state has shown greater progress in the development of its natural resources.

Probably no state has greater resources capable of development. The coal beds of Eastern Kentucky comprise an area of more than ten thousand square miles or about one-fourth the area of the whole state, and the western coal fields underlie four thousand square miles, or about one-tenth of the area of the state. Inexhaustible deposits of iron ore are found, and the forests are exceedingly rich in fine lumber.

The state has made wonderful progress in the development of the school system. In fact, no other state has a more practical and efficient school system, nor has any state a more determined set of school workers.

Kentucky has had three permanent Capitol buildings. The last was completed in 1909 at a cost of $1,750,000, and is considered one of the handsomest structures of its kind in the Union.

Great virtues are sometimes accompanied by great faults; but Kentucky's faults have been those born of isolation and inaccessibility. Now that her railways are penetrating into even the remotest districts, bringing her citizens into closer and quicker communication with the outside world, her people rapidly are becoming united in their efforts to make her future eclipse her glorious past. With the purest Anglo-Saxon blood in the United States forming the greater part of her citizenship, and the riches of her forests and mountains even now just beginning to pour into the laps of the people, a great future is inevitable for Kentucky, "The land of the China Brier."

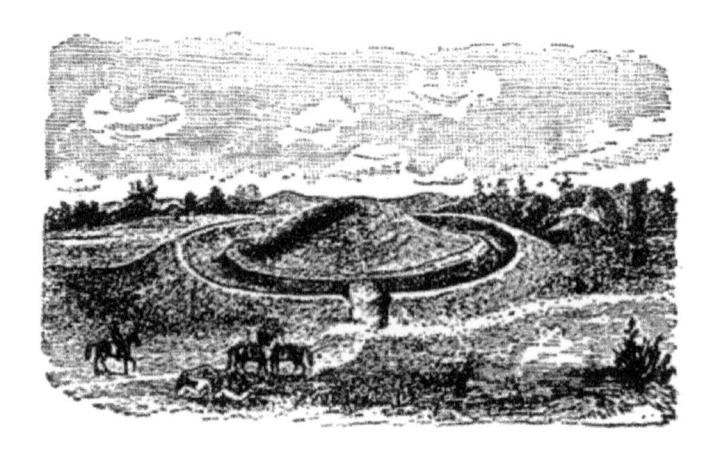

Ancient Mound, Greenup County